# MORNINGS WITH MOMMY

Written by Astere Yemmer          Art by Mariia Luzina

To all of the families, including my own,
that found themselves in a sudden whirlwind of heartache in 2020.
May you find the rainbow after the storm!

Teachable Moment: What does it mean for your ears to open? Is it the same as opening your eyes?

Ears slowly opening, my eyes remain closed. The smell of coffee lingers, seeping slowly into my nose.

When something "lingers", it stays around for a while. It is clear that the main character is familiar with this smell.

I begin to stretch my left arm.
Then I stretch my right.

I pull my stuffy close to me.

It keeps me company through the night.

I hear familiar rumblings, far beyond

my bedroom door.

Teachable Moment: When something "rumbles", it makes a deep sound. When something is "faint", you can barely hear it.

A click-clack in the hallway. A faint growl, I recognize as a snore.

"Click-Clack" makes the sound of footsteps. This is a figurative language tool called Onomatopoeia.

I think it's been long enough now. I slowly get down out of my bed.

Memories of yesterday begin
to take shape inside of my head.

Walking toward my parents' room, I notice the door is ajar.

Teachable Moment: What do you think the word "ajar" means?

"Mommy!" I whisper in my sleepy-sounding voice. Her response to me comes from afar.

The familiar slippers are missing.

Fur filled black, white, and red.

The covers shift ever-so-slightly.
This lets me know that Pops is fast asleep.

BETTER togeter

Teachable Moment: What kind of movements do you think of when you hear the word "creep" to describe how the main character is leaving he parent's bedroom?

Backing out of their bedroom slowly, I take each step in a "tip-toe" creep.

Turning on my heels,
I look up toward the door
and past the staircase.

"Good morning Almaz!" My mommy says as she extends her arms, pulling me in real close.

Teachable Moment: The word "extends" means to hold out toward someone.

"How about some almond milk with your favorite breakfast meal..." I squeal, "French toast?"

What is your favorite breakfast meal?

As we walk downstairs, I think of the mornings when we had to get dressed to go outside.

Every morning mommy called for me,

but for more sleep... I often cried.

Pops was always the first one dressed and ready to be on his way.

My brother usually took the longest to leave, running out of the house each day.

Mommy and I would ride together,

her to teach, and I to learn at school.

Her school building was right next to mine,

a fact I always thought was pretty cool!

But now, my parents work from home. My brother and I learn remotely, so no-one has to leave.

Teachable Moment: Learning remotely means you do not go into the school building to have classes.

We each have time for rest and play, but only after our lessons because there is still much to achieve.

The word "achieve" means to get something by working hard for it.

The change to our lives happened in March 2020 because of a virus called Covid-19.

Lots of people got sick, so doctors and lawmakers said, to stay safe, we should stay home and quarantine.

ONAVIRUS  4:22  43°  4 NEW YORK

Teachable Moment: "Quarantine" means that you must be separated from others so that a virus does not spread.

So now I wake up a little later for school,

but mommy is still up early to prepare.

I brush my teeth, put on my uniform,

and mommy helps me fix my hair.

Teachable Moment: When you "prepare" for something, you are getting ready for it.

What do you think the main character's mommy is preparing for?

She takes lots of notes, sips from her elephant mug, and rubs my shoulder in her mommy-like way.

At 9 a.m. my school day begins.

My teacher posts our assignments and

we meet for class on Zoom.

On Friday's my mommy makes me a snack for my lunch party, and I chat with classmates in a special "breakout" room.

Teachable Moment: A "breakout room" is not an actual room that you walk into. It is a virtual room used when on a computer.

I know that things are different now, and our days and nights don't look quite the same.

I have much more time to spend with my family, watching movies or playing a fun board game.

Teachable Moment: What is something that you enjoy doing with your family?

We sit around the table for dinner and share thoughts about our day as evening turns to night,

and somehow,

someway this new way of life,

to me... feels just right!

I know that one day things may

go back to the way that

they always were.

Astere Yemmer resides in the Bronx, New York with her husband and two children. Astere has been an educator for 14 years, she is a Virginia State University Alum, attends the Abyssinian Baptist Church in Harlem, and is an active member of The Bronx Alumnae Chapter of Delta Sigma Theta Sorority Incorporated. Astere comes from a family of educators and has taught children and coached adults for many years. Mornings With Mommy is Astere's second book, and it is based on her family's experience during the Covid-19 pandemic.

Mariia Luzina was born in Ukraine in the small city of Kryvyj Rih. She lived with her grandparents until she was 15 when she immigrated to Italy to live with her mother. Mariia has always loved to draw and even went to an Art School when she was a child. It was a hobby until the age of 20 when her best friend told her about an opportunity to become an illustrator for children's books. She decided to give it a try and has worked with several authors since that time.